HOPE RISING

When Life Makes Faith Difficult

Gene Appel

EASTSIDE CHRISTIAN CHURCH

Hope Rising was written and produced
by Lifetogether Ministries in Lake
Forest, California. Founded in 1992 by
Brett Eastman who served as the
Small Group Champion for over
10 years at both Willow Creek and
Saddleback Church, Lifetogether
is a ministry committed to helping
local churches connect their entire
congregations into community in order
to reach their community for Christ. For
over 12 years, Lifetogether has helped
to produce hundreds of custom dvd
small group curriculum and church
wide small group campaigns for
churches all around the country. For
more information on producing your
own campaign and curriculum go to
Lifetogether.com

Table of Contents

Contents

Appendix

Small Group Leaders

About The Author

Endorsements

"Everyone needs hope. But what do you do when you find yourself without it? *Hope Rising* will encourage you to hold on to the hope that Christ has for us."

**Craig Groeschel,
Senior Pastor of LifeChurch.tv, Author of Altar Ego, Becoming Who God Says You Are**

"Everybody needs hope. *Hope Rising* is an authentic and gutsy dealing with life, faith and God; especially so when some things are not making sense. I love Gene Appel. I love his heart and I love the way that he treats complex issues with insight, sensitivity and integrity. He speaks as one who has tasted pain but without the negative residue. There is something very powerful about people sharing their stories, too. *Hope Rising* will birth hope in many who desperately long for it and feel like it is in short supply."

**Dale Stevenson,
Senior Pastor, Crossway Baptist Church, Melbourne, Australia**

"You know restaurants, movies and sports teams all can get vastly over-rated, but not so with hope. That's why I'm so excited about this series! My buddy Gene Appel knows as much about hanging onto hope through the challenges of life as anybody I know. He'd be the first to tell you that there are a lot of things in life that are over-rated, but HOPE is not one of them!"

**Mike Breaux,
Author and Teaching Pastor, Heartland Community Church, Rockford, IL**

"Everyone needs hope. Without it we curl up and die. With it the giants in our lives can be faced up to and conquered. *Hope Rising* will remind you of the power and reason for the hope that we have in Christ. This is a message that can change you and your church. I recommend it."

**Larry Osborne,
Author and Pastor, North Coast Church, Vista, CA**

"I'm so excited that the series *Hope Rising* has found it's way into your hands. In a world full of challenges, disappointment, fear, loss, injustice and pain we all need to know that there is still hope. Without hope we would certainly give up. Without hope we would not have the courage to rise up. Without hope we would not have the strength to speak up. For those feeling hopeless, my prayer is that this series will leave you filled with hope!"

Christine Caine,
Founder of The A21 Campaign

"After I watched this video series , my first thought was 'At last!' The stories in *Hope Rising* will awaken your own stories. Each one is a story of triumph and tragedy that will inspire you to believe that God is most obviously present even when he seems apparently absent. Gene's teaching let me know that there's someone who truly understands that God's strength is made perfect in our imperfections. This is a resource you'll go back to again and again."

Pete Wilson,
Senior Pastor of CrossPoint Church, Nashville, TN

"My friend Gene Appel is an encourager, communicator and teacher whose message of hope will strengthen your faith and elevate your life. *Hope Rising* presents a living message that will enable you to overcome difficult circumstances with the confident expectation that your future is in God's Hands."

Jack Graham,
Pastor of Prestonwood Baptist Church, Plano, TX

"*HOPE RISING* is a powerful and creative answer to life's difficult questions about faith and humanity. Gene Appel has assembled stories of real sojourners who've traveled the uneven roads and now have gathered to offer a tangible hope to others on the same passage. If you need not only answers but understanding, this is for you. "

Wayne Cordeiro,
Author and Pastor New Hope Christian Fellowship

"Gene Appel is a fantastic communicator who insightfully guides us to the power of hope, and the One who gives it. *Hope Rising* speaks straight to our fears, concerns, and worries and offers us more than a cliché but a profound living hope that can sustain us through all of life's ups and downs. Gene's teaching, along with the many stories of life change, are an incredible gift to us all."

Jud Wilhite,
Author of Pursued, Senior Pastor of Central Christian Church,
Las Vegas, NV

"Gene Appel has done a fantastic job tackling one of the most important topics that any of us will ever ponder. Hope. It's the thing that if we have it, we feel very alive, and if we lose it, we seem to lose our very being. That's why I love this series. It's an awesome reminder that if we'll allow it, we will experience *Hope Rising*!"

Lincoln Brewster,
Integrity Music Recording Artist and Worship Arts Pastor at
Bayside Church, Granite Bay, CA

"Gene Appel has done it again—this time with captivating teaching, quality resources, real life testimonies and Bible truths that will change your outlook on life. *Hope Rising*...is a project done with excellence that will help you feel encouraged when you face the valleys of life."

Pastor Dave Stone,
Southeast Christian Church, Louisville, KY

"In a world desperate for hope, *Hope Rising* offers the paradox of a hope found in arms stretched wide on a cross. Those who embrace the source of this *Hope Rising* will find that it will carry them through every broken dream, every deep sorrow, every dark place until one day those same arms are again spread wide to welcome them safely home to the very real Hope of heaven."

Dr. Carol Taylor,
President of Vanguard University

"These messages promise to touch hearts, stir hope and change lives. In an era of bad news, this effort is a welcome silver lining."

Max Lucado,
Author and Pastor

"*Hope Rising* offers exactly what is needed when life doesn't turn out the way you planned or expected. In this video series, Gene Appel brings his extraordinary Bible teaching skills alongside remarkable true stories to offer what we all need most – hope! I highly recommend *Hope Rising*; it will not only provide motivation to get you through the day, but inspire you to look expectantly toward your future!"

Dave Ferguson,
Lead Pastor - Community Christian Church Spiritual
Entrepreneur – NewThing

"If organizational cultures are created by the stories we tell and the heroes we create, then *HOPE RISING* may be one of the most powerful shapers. If personal lives are deeply transformed by raw and authentic hope springing up in the midst of pain, confusion and anger, then *HOPE RISING* is what we need. In a real, open and creative way these stories will provoke you, wound you, and heal you with their hope in the living God."

Nancy Ortberg,
Author of Non-Linear Leadership

"You hold in your hands a catalyst for hope, a future, and a fresh start. We know firsthand Gene Appel and the Eastside team are hope givers and we believe in what they are doing. Get ready to experience hope in a fresh dimension."

Paul Jr. and Rachael Teutul,
Paul Jr. Designs, Stars of American Chopper, Discovery Channel

Foreword

The most powerful force in the world is not generated by splitting atoms or focusing lasers. It lies beyond the control of any technology, the price of any corporation or the control of any government. The most powerful force in the world is available to its poorest citizen. It has no cost, although desperate people would pay anything for it. It has no known limits, although those who lack it would travel anywhere to find it.

It is called hope. And hope is rising. A friend of mine, the best marriage expert I know, said that when he counseled couples his goal was simply to help them experience ten percent improvement. Because if they could do that—no matter how bad their marriage had been—they would taste hope. And once someone tastes hope, all bets are off. Anything can happen.

Hope springs eternal. It's hope that keeps young couples seeking to give birth to new little lives even though our world can be such a mess. It's hope that brings every baseball team back to spring training. It's hope that keeps courageous young children battling against foes as difficult as cancer. Hope is there at the beginning of every marriage, at the birth of every business, at the launch of every friendship, at the commencement of the most long-shot dream. Human beings can survive almost anything. But we cannot outlive our hope.

A wise writer said that human beings have three strategies for coping with the disappointments that are inevitable to life in this world. One is despair—to continue to want, but to believe what I want will never come to fruition. Human beings cannot last long in despair. Another strategy is resignation. In resignation, I try to cope by convincing myself that I don't really want my heart's desire after all. Then there is hope. Hope means I keep wanting, and I trust that something better is coming.

The Bible is the great book of hope. Paul does not say: "May the God of all Resignation fill you with Resignation..." God is the God of hope.

You are about to become a student of hope. Gene Appel and Eastside are in the hope distribution business. And when all our immediate hopes for this or that outcome fail (and sooner or later they all will), every human being needs a fall-back hope, a foundational hope, an ultimate hope.
There is only One. So join in, read, study, talk, think, pray....and hope.
Hope is rising.

- John Ortberg

Acknowledgements

Pulling together a creative curriculum and creating the kind of resource you hold in your hand and the accompanying DVD doesn't just happen.

Brett Eastman, Allen White and the team from LifeTogether have been encouraging, creative, passionate partners who brought an enormous deal of energy and guidance to this project at every step of the way. We could not have done it without them.

Jill Gille, Korry Ashton, and Jan Lynn brought their professional and production expertise in capturing the stories and teaching on top of already full schedules and worked their usual magic.

We can't do anything at Eastside without feeling the support, protection, and the big picture vision of our elder board who undergird all our ministries and efforts and are the most supportive group of leaders on the planet.

The unsung heroes are the Connection and Small Group leaders who inspire us to resource and bless their contributions with resources like this as they create environments for thousands to belong, grow and serve.

Finally, a special word of appreciation goes to the staff of Eastside who, with great vulnerability, shared their personal stories on the *Hope Rising* DVD. These are not just Hope Givers doing a video project, but these are people who give hope to thousands of people every day as they selflessly advance God's work in the hearts and lives of people.

Introduction

Greetings! You're going to watch and hear me say a number of times in the weeks to come that I am very glad you have decided to participate in this small group series. Perhaps this is your first venture into this kind of personal exposure. Let me tell you right from the start that you have already put yourself in a place where you can actually see hope start rising in your situation, wherever you find yourself right now! You have created space for God to work in your life by that decision to get with a few others and learn, live and grow together. Welcome!

I realize I can't ask you to be self-disclosing with others in your small group if I'm not willing to do that with you. So I'm going to be as transparent as I know how in the context of the issues we'll be talking about in this series. It's not that I like to admit my failures and shortcomings; it's that I know from experience that if we're unwilling to share where we've gone off the track with people who care for us, we can't know the joy of discovering they can help us get back on track and can pray for us as we realize God is at work on us along the way!

These weeks may not be easy, but they will be healthy for us. Any change of bad habits or wrong behavior feels awkward at first. I know this firsthand. But unless we can see what's holding hope down and take some consistent steps forward we're not going to see hope rising the way God intends it to in our lives. And I'm praying more than anything else that in various ways during these weeks you will definitely see hope rising in your soul, in your mind and in your life.

I've really enjoyed preparing these sessions and I'm looking forward to spending the next few weeks with you. I want to thank you up front for your time. I believe your discussions throughout *Hope Rising* could potentially be among the most powerful you've ever experienced. They could mark a significant turning point in your life. But you'll have to decide that six weeks from now. For this moment, we hope you enjoy your time together, creating space for God to work and observe hope rising.

Gene

Using this Workbook

1. Notice in the Table of Contents there are three sections: (1) Sessions; (2) Appendix; and (3) Small Group Leaders. Familiarize yourself with the Appendix parts. Some of them will be used in the sessions themselves.

2. If you are facilitating/leading or co-leading a small group, the section Small Group Leaders will give you some hard-learned experiences of others that will encourage you and help you avoid many common obstacles to effective small group leadership.

3. Use this workbook as a guide, not a straightjacket. If the group responds to the lesson in an unexpected but honest way, go with that. If you think of a better question than the next one in the lesson, ask it. Take to heart the insights included in the Frequently Asked Questions pages and the Small Group Leaders section.

4. Enjoy your small group experience.

5. Now read the Outline of Each Session on the next pages so that you understand how the sessions will flow.

Outline of Each Session

Most people want to live a life that is orderly, meaningful and satisfying, but few achieve this by themselves. And most small groups struggle to balance all of God's purposes in their meetings. Groups tend to overemphasize one of the various reasons for meeting. Rarely is there a healthy balance that includes teaching, evangelism, ministry, practical exercises and worship. That's why we've included all of these elements in this study so you can live a healthy, balanced spiritual life over time.

A typical group session for *Hope Rising* will include the following:

THEME.

The lessons we will learn during *Hope Rising* are best illustrated in the lives of real people. Each session's teaching will include comments by real people reflecting on the significance of the theme for that session in their lives.

COMING TOGETHER.

The foundation for spiritual growth is an intimate connection with God and his family. A few people who really know you and who earn your trust provide a place to experience the life Jesus invites you to live. This section of each session typically offers you two options. You can get to know your whole group by using the icebreaker question(s), or you can check

in with one or two group members— your spiritual partner(s)—for a deeper connection and encouragement in your spiritual journey.

As your group begins, use the Small Group Agreement, Small Group Calendar, and Purpose Team Roles to help your group see how everyone has a part in making a small group come to life. As the group develops intimacy, use the Spiritual Partner's Check-In Page and Prayer and Praise Report to keep the group connected.

LEARNING TOGETHER/DVD TEACHING SEGMENT.

Serving as a companion to the *Hope Rising* small group discussion book is the *Hope Rising* Video teaching. This DVD is designed to combine teaching segments from Pastor Gene along with leadership insights and personal stories of life change. Using the teaching video will add value to this six week commitment of doing life together and help you discover how walking with Christ changes everything.

GROWING TOGETHER.

Here is where you will process as a group the teaching you heard and saw. The focus won't be on accumulating information but on how we should live in light of the Word of God. We want to help you apply the insights from Scripture practically, creatively and from your heart as well as your head. At the end of the day, allowing the timeless truths from God's Word to transform our lives in Christ is our greatest aim.

GOING DEEPER.

If you have time and want to dig deeper into more Bible passages about the topic at hand, we've provided additional passages and questions. Your group may choose to do study homework ahead of each meeting in order to cover more biblical material. If you prefer not to do study homework, the Going Deeper section will provide you with plenty to discuss within the group. These options allow individuals or the whole group to expand their study, while still accommodating those who can't do homework or are new to your group.

SHARING TOGETHER.

Here we let the truth we are learning travel the 18 inches from our cranium (mind) to our cardium (heart, emotions and will). Here is where the Bible urging us to ""Do not merely listen to the word..." (James 1:22) comes into play. Many people skip over this aspect of the Christian life because it's scary, relationally awkward or simply too much work for their busy schedules. But Jesus wanted all of His disciples to help outsiders connect with Him, to know Him personally, and to carry out His commands. This doesn't necessarily mean preaching on street corners. It could mean welcoming a few newcomers into your group, hosting a short-term group in your home or walking through this study with a friend. In this study, you'll have an opportunity to go beyond Bible study to biblical living.

GOING TOGETHER.

We have Jesus' affirmation that every aspect of life can ultimately be measured as a way of fulfilling one or both of the "bottom line" commandments: "The most important one," answered Jesus, "is this: 'Hear, O Israel, the Lord our God, the Lord is one. Love the Lord your God with all your heart and with all your soul and with all your mind and with all your strength.' The second is this: 'Love your neighbor as yourself.' There is no commandment greater than these" (Mark 12:29–31 NIV). The group session will close with time for personal response to God and group prayer, seeking to keep this crucial commandments before us at all times.

This is a good place to have different group members close in prayer, even when the instructions don't specify. You can also provide some time, if the schedule allows, for people to reflect on their Prayer and Praise Report or take a little time to meet with a Spiritual Partner.

DAILY REFLECTIONS.

Each week on the Daily Reflections pages we provide scriptures to read and reflect on between group meetings. We suggest you use this section to seek God on your own throughout the week. This time at home should begin and end with prayer. Don't get in a hurry; take enough time to hear God's direction.

WEEKLY MEMORY VERSES.

For each session we have provided a Memory Verse that emphasizes an important truth from the session. This is an optional exercise, but we believe that memorizing Scripture can be a vital part of filling our minds with God's will for our lives. We encourage you to give this important habit a try.

Sooner or later we're going to discover, each in our own way, that life won't go the way we planned. Sometimes better; sometimes much worse. But in this session and the rest of this study we are going to discover what God does with that moment when we find out that our plans were limited compared to His great plan for us!

Session 1

When Life Doesn't Go the Way You Planned

Welcome to Hope Rising! Enjoy the company around you on this brief journey and remember that the next few weeks are a short chapter in a larger story God is writing in your life. Let's discover together what it means to live in such a way that steps we take keep hope rising no matter what obstacles we encounter.

Hope is a big deal. We need it. It's one of the parts of life that we can honestly say we never have enough of. You've probably never heard someone say, "I've got all the hope I need. My hope tank is completely full and overflowing." Most of us face each day looking for a little more hope. And one of the things about others that we find fascinating is when we notice they are hopeful. We want to know what gives them hope. We long to figure out if where they find hope is a place we can find hope, too.

Hope is Rising

It would be our prayer that in the weeks to come you will gradually notice the level of hope rising in your life and in the lives around you. And one of the ways we're going to approach this is by looking at some of the aspects of life that drain our hope or let us know we might have been trusting in something that couldn't sustain hope.

Coming Together

During each session, we will begin with a question or brief activity designed to "put us on the same page" for the session. Since this is your first time together (at least for this new series), take a few minutes to make sure everyone knows names. You may want to review briefly the Small Group Agreement and Calendar from the Appendix.

1 As you begin, take time to pass around a copy of the Small Group Roster on page 101, a sheet of paper, or have someone pass a Study Guide, opened to the Small Group Roster. Have everyone write down their contact information. Ask someone to make copies or type up a list with everyone's information and email it to the group this week.

2 As you can tell by the title of this series, we're going to talk about hope in the next few weeks. Let's begin by brainstorming some definitions of hope. What is hope? What examples of hope come to mind right away?

3 Whether your group is new or ongoing, it's always important to reflect on and review your values together. On page 94 is a Small Group Agreement with the values we've found most useful in sustaining healthy, balanced groups. We recommend that you choose one or two values—ones you haven't previously focused on or have room to grow in—to emphasize during this study. Choose ones that will take your group to the next stage of intimacy and spiritual health.

- If your group is new, you may want to focus on welcoming newcomers or on sharing group ownership. Any group will quickly move from being the leader's group to our group if everyone understands the goals of the group and shares a small role. See the Purpose Team Roles in Appendix for help on how to do this well.

- We recommend that you rotate host homes on a regular basis and let the hosts lead the meeting. We've come to realize that healthy groups rotate leadership. This helps to develop every member's ability to shepherd a few people in a safe environment. Even Jesus gave others the opportunity to serve alongside him (Mark 6:30–44). Look at the FAQs in the Appendix for additional information about hosting or leading the group.

LEARNING TOGETHER

Use the space below for notes, questions or comments you want to bring up in the discussion later.

Growing Together

In the questions that follow, you will review and expand on the teaching you just experienced.

4 Thinking about the opening stories you heard in the video, what did you learn about hope?

5 Gene made the point that we are all "irrepressible hopers." He mentioned marriage and children as examples. What other examples can you think of that demonstrate our tendency to hope?

6 Gene asked a probing question we should talk about for a few moments here at the beginning: "What happens in people's lives when things don't go the way they expected them to go?" How do people cope with those kinds of disappointment?

7 Luke 24:13-32 includes the account of Jesus meeting two disciples on the road to Emmaus the same day He rose from the grave. Gene quoted verse 21 in which the men tell Jesus about the disappointment caused by His death: "But we had hoped that he was the one who was going to redeem Israel. And what is more, it is the third day since all this took place" (NIV2011). What kind of hope were they talking about?

8 So far in this session we've been talking about hope in general terms and related to areas of ordinary life. How does hope affect the spiritual area of life?

9 Gene described the incident with the young man who gave him a .22 bullet. What objects have you come across that represent hope perhaps in an unusual way for you or someone else?

10 Did you relate with Gene's final point that sometimes hope is right under your nose? In what ways?

Going Deeper

You can explore the following Bible passages behind the teaching for this session as a group (if there is time) or on your own between sessions.

Read Luke 24:13-32. Gene used part of this event in Jesus' life to illustrate the significance of hope in our lives. Let's look at the entire event for even more clues about the importance of others in our lives as part of an active and effective faith.

- Why do you think Jesus held back from immediately identifying Himself to these two men?

- Verses 19-24 record the disciples' "testimony" about Jesus. What did they get right and what did they get wrong?

- Verses 25-27 records Jesus' response and teaching. What didn't He talk about?

- Why do you think they recognized Him when He broke bread?

- How do you think this entire event affected the hope awareness of these two men? What did they do as a result?

Sharing Together

Now it's time to make some personal applications to all we've been thinking about in the last few minutes.

11 Gene pointed out that hope is one way of describing what we expect or dream will happen. When those results don't come about, our lives and outlook are challenged and sometimes crushed. In what situations has your hope taken a serious blow?

12 What places of your life would you be willing to consider may be "out of control" right now, to use Gene's phrase to describe a loss of hope?

13 How would you connect your understanding of hope in the largest sense with your understanding of Jesus Christ and his unique role?

Going Together

During these sessions we are doing things "together:" learning, thinking, growing, praying, choosing, etc. Part of "together" is how we live when we aren't together. Here are some questions to clarify our shared purposes until we meet again.

14 Part of the "together" style of these sessions is an emphasis on seeking and welcoming new people to the group. Who might you invite to join us for these sessions? If someone came to mind, write their name(s) here:

15 Allow everyone to answer this question: "How can we pray for you this week?" Be sure to write prayer requests on your Prayer and Praise Report on page 100.

Close the session in prayer. Encourage each other to pray for others in the group.

Daily Reflections

These are daily reviews of the key Bible verses and related others that will help you think about and apply the insights from this session.

Day 1

Ecclesiastes 3:1 | Time for what Matters

There is a time for everything, and a season for every activity under the heavens. (NIV2011)

How does this verse point to reasonable hope in life?

Day 2

Acts 17:27 | Sought Seekers

God did this so that they would seek him and perhaps reach out for him and find him, though he is not far from any one of us. Acts 17:27 (NIV2011)

What does this verse say to you about Gene's point that sometimes the hope found in Jesus is right under our noses?

Day 3

Ecclesiastes 3:11 | Hope towards Eternity

He has made everything beautiful in its time. He has also set eternity in the human heart; yet no one can fathom what God has done from beginning to end. (NIV2011)

In what sense do you identify with that phrase "eternity in the heart" in your life and how does it affect your understanding of hope?

Day 4

1 Peter 3:15 | *Reason for Hope*

But in your hearts revere Christ as Lord. Always be prepared to give an answer to everyone who asks you to give the reason for the hope that you have. But do this with gentleness and respect. (NIV2011)

What is the strongest reason for hope in your life?

Day 5

Luke 24:32 | *Side Effects of Hope*

They asked each other, "Were not our hearts burning within us while he talked with us on the road and opened the Scriptures to us?" (NIV2011)

What was it about that conversation that caused the disciples' hearts to burn?

Weekly Memory Verse

But in your hearts revere Christ as Lord. Always be prepared to give an answer to everyone who asks you to give the reason for the hope that you have. But do this with gentleness and respect.
(1 Peter 3:15 NIV2011)

In this session, Phil, Phylicia and Dave will help us identify what it feels like when life is out of control. It isn't always obvious. We can get so wrapped up in the busy-ness, the mesmerizing flash of life going by that we don't see the signs that our vehicle is out of control.

Session 2

When the Speed of Life Is Out of Control

Welcome to week two of Hope Rising! This time we get to explore the side effects of dashed hopes and hopeless causes. It's so easy to get wrapped up in a busy life that we lose all sense that what we're doing is taking a toll on us and not accomplishing what God wants in the long run.

There's something intoxicating about speed! The child on the playground merry-go-round squeals, "Faster, Daddy, faster!" Not that much later, as a teenager out for her first drive alone in Daddy's car, she finds it almost irresistible to mash the pedal to the floor to see the world flashing by. We all sometimes echo the words of the pilot in the movie Top Gun: "I feel the need…the need for speed." We hardly think about all the ways we can read the bumper sticker on the car we flash by on the highway that suggests: Speed Kills.

Hope is Rising.

As we will see in *Hope Rising*, before we can start making the kinds of changes that will make a huge difference in our lives we may have to identify why our lives are out of control. We're going to start with speed and time. How we are pacing and prioritizing life will tell us a lot about the condition of our lives. But here's the test: it doesn't matter what we say is important to us if we don't make time for it. What we make time for is what's really important to us. How much time we make for God says a lot about our relationship with Him. The pace of our other relationships speaks volumes about what they mean to us.

Coming Together

During each session, we will begin with a question or brief activity designed to "put us on the same page" for the session. Continue to make sure everyone knows names.

1 There are many ways to experience speed. And sometimes the sensation of speed is greater even when we aren't actually going all that fast. For example, what feels faster—going 100 mph in a car or 25 mph in the front of a roller coaster taking the long plunge? What's your most vivid memory of speed? Describe what it was like.

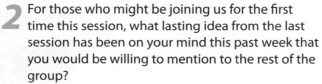

2 For those who might be joining us for the first time this session, what lasting idea from the last session has been on your mind this past week that you would be willing to mention to the rest of the group?

LEARNING TOGETHER

Use the space below for notes, questions or comments you want to bring up in the discussion later.

Growing Together

In the questions that follow, you will review and expand on the teaching you just experienced.

3 How did you relate to the opening montage of hope-centered stories before the teaching? What parallels can you think of from your own life?

4 Gene illustrated the fast pace of life by using his own experience early in marriage. In what areas of life do you most recognize things are moving fast—maybe out of control?

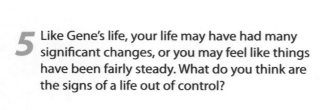

5 Like Gene's life, your life may have had many significant changes, or you may feel like things have been fairly steady. What do you think are the signs of a life out of control?

6 Think for a minute about King David in the Old Testament at the top of his game (2 Samuel 11—12). He was doing his own thing, and basically accountable to no one. When he was attracted to a married woman named Bathsheba, he took her. Then things began to spin out of control, ending up with the murder of Bathsheba's husband and David bringing the now pregnant widow to his palace. Enter a friend named Nathan, a friend like Gene's friend Eddie.

Why does it often take someone else to speak into our lives and say, "You're out of control. It's time to make it right"?

7 Based on what Gene mentioned about Eddie, his buddies and Barb's intervention, how did they exercise accountability in Gene's life?

8 How did Gene respond, at first, to the truth he was being shown about his own life? Why do you think he felt that way?

9 What were some of the factors that led Gene eventually to admit he was deeply thankful that his wife and friends had come after him when his life was out of control?

10 What do you think it takes for a gathering of strangers or slight acquaintances to become a small group where people hold each other accountable in healthy ways? Why are such relationships healthy for us?

11 Gene ended his teaching with an invitation to "take the masks off a little" and work on honesty about the pace of our lives. Why do you think it's hard for us to do this?

Going Deeper

You can explore the following Bible passages behind the teaching for this session as a group (if there is time) or on your own between sessions.

Read Psalm 23:1-6. Gene mentioned this Psalm in his closing. In this entire Psalm, David examines both his relationship with God and the amazing evidence of God's care for him. David is meditating on a sheep's pace of life in this song:

- Identify some of the ways you see David letting God shape the pace of his life in this Psalm. How do you understand the importance of having God restore your soul (v.3)?

- What benefits do you see happening in the Psalm that can only happen when a person recognizes how God wants our lives to be different than those around us?

- If God was acting as your Shepherd, where would you expect Him to make changes in the way you live?

Read Romans 12:1-21. This is the part of his letter to the Romans where Paul launches into very practical instructions. He begins with "Therefore," basically saying, "If everything I said in chapters 1-11 is true, then here's how to make room for it to be true in your life":

- How does the description of "living sacrifices" picture a life that seeks God's design for living?

- The theme of verses 3-8 is service and the way God makes it possible for each of us to serve others in a unique way. How might service to others bring a sense of balance to a life out of control?

• Verses 9-21 are a series of small obediences, specific ways we can behave as God wants us to behave. Which one or two of these do you think would create a significant change of pace in your life that would allow God to work if you put it into practice?

Sharing Together

Now it's time to make some personal applications to all we've been thinking about in the last few minutes.

12 If a normal speed of life could be described as 55 miles per hour, what speed would you assign to your current lifestyle?

13 In what specific area(s) do you sense God calling you to take your foot off the pedal? How will your choices affect those areas?

14 If you could put into words one new personal idea or challenge you are taking from this session, what would it be? How did the interview with various people at the beginning of the DVD impact your understanding of letting God begin to determine the speed of your life?

Going Together

During these sessions we are doing things "together:" learning, thinking, growing, praying, choosing, etc. Part of together is how we live when we aren't together. Here are some questions to clarify our shared purposes until we meet again.

15 What's one idea from this session you plan to talk about with someone beyond this group this week? Why?

16 Take a look at the Circles of Life diagram below and write the names of two or three people you know who need to experience a new or deeper relationship with Christ. Commit to praying for God's guidance and an opportunity to share with each of them.

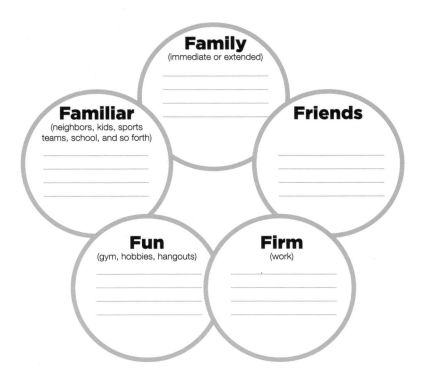

Family
(immediate or extended)

Familiar
(neighbors, kids, sports teams, school, and so forth)

Friends

Fun
(gym, hobbies, hangouts)

Firm
(work)

17 Pair up with someone in your group. (We suggest that men partner with men and women with women.) This person will be your spiritual partner for the rest of this study. He or she doesn't have to be your best friend, but will simply encourage you to complete the goals you set for yourself during this study. Following through on a resolution is tough when you're on your own, but we've found it makes all the difference to have a partner cheering us on.

Let's close in prayer, taking turns praying specifically for others in the group and beyond.

Daily Reflections

These are daily reviews of the key Bible verses and related others that will help you think about and apply the insights from this session.

Day 1

Psalm 23:1-2 | A Sheep's Life
The LORD is my shepherd, I lack nothing...
He makes me lie down in green pastures, he leads me beside quiet waters.
(NIV2011)

How are you presently experiencing God's shepherding role in your life?

Day 2

Psalm 23:3 | Hope Rising from Soul Restoration
...he refreshes my soul. He guides me along the right paths for his name's sake.
(NIV2011)

In what ways can you describe the way God refreshes/restores your soul?

Day 3

Psalm 23:4 | The Pace in the Valley
Even though I walk through the darkest valley, I will fear no evil, for you are with me; your rod and your staff, they comfort me. (NIV2011)

Do you think the psalmist is describing the place where we live or situations we occasionally pass through? What pace of life is he describing?

Day 4
Psalm 23:5 | Table, Oil and Cup
You prepare a table before me in the presence of my enemies. You anoint my head with oil; my cup overflows. (NIV2011)

How do each of the items mentioned (table, oil and cup) represent aspects of your relationship with Christ?

Day 5
Psalm 23:6 | Everlasting Hope
Surely your goodness and love will follow me all the days of my life, and I will dwell in the house of the LORD forever. (NIV2011)

In what ways does this verse describe your understanding of the hope God offers us in Christ?

Weekly Memory Verse

The LORD is my shepherd, I lack nothing.
He makes me lie down in green pastures, he
leads me beside quiet waters, he refreshes
my soul. He guides me along the right paths
for his name's sake.
Psalm 23:1-3 (NIV2011)

The theme for this session is disappointment with the hand we're dealt. Jim, Greg and Bill will give us some insight into how we can all identify with the feelings of loss, disappointment and despair in response to how life is unfolding. But many of us need to realize that the hand we're dealt doesn't look or feel right because we're in the wrong "game" and we need to get to the table of reality.

Session 3

When You Are Not Happy with the Hand You Are Dealt

In the last session, Gene mentioned the great breakfast deal he and his buddies shared regularly at one of the Vegas Casinos. Hanging around those establishments clearly caused him to pick up some of the terminology, too. If life is seen as some kind of card game, it's easy to think that the hand we've been dealt to play and even the extra cards that come to us aren't fair or what we asked for.

Hope is Rising.

When our hand seems lousy, what happens to our hope? Most of us don't readily discount God's role in the dealing out of life, but we wonder sometimes if He's stacked the deck against us or if He even cares how He shuffles and passes out the "cards." Ultimately, we have to get clear on whether our hope rests in the hand that is dealt to us or the hand that deals life.

Coming Together

During each session, we begin with a question or brief activity designed to "put us on the same page" for the session.

1 Time for everyone to come clean. What's your favorite card or board game and why do you like it?

2 For the benefit of those who might be joining us for the first time this session, who would like to describe one significant discovery you've made in the first two sessions that is already making a difference in your life?

3 Rotating leaders is one of the group values we highly recommend for your group. People need opportunities to experiment with ways in which God may have gifted them. Your group will give you all the encouragement you need before, during and after the session.

We also suggest you rotate host homes, with the host of each meeting providing the refreshments. Some groups like to let the host lead the meeting each week, while others like to let one person host while another person leads.

The Small Group Calendar on page 95 is a tool for planning who will host and lead each meeting. Take a few minutes to plan hosts and leaders for your remaining meetings. Don't pass this up! It will revolutionize your group.

LEARNING TOGETHER

Use the space below for notes, questions or comments you want to bring up in the discussion later.

Growing Together

In the questions that follow, you will review and expand on the teaching you just experienced.

4 Gene gave a few of the highlights from the biography of Joseph in the Old Testament (not the Joseph who was married to Mary, the mother of Jesus). The details are actually found in Genesis 37—50. By way of group review, who can remember an event or factoid about Joseph' life?

5 Think about the "hand" Joseph ended up holding the day before he was summoned to Pharaoh's palace. He had been betrayed and then sold into slavery by his brothers, earned great responsibility in his master's house only to be abused and then betrayed by the master's wife, rejected and imprisoned by the master, made himself useful in prison and helped other prisoners only to be apparently forgotten. What kinds of similar situations tend to make you want to "fold" your hand and quit the game?

6 What do you think kept Joseph going against all the odds?

7 Gene talked about the hidden lake his family loves to visit for fishing. Can you relate to that story in some other area of life? Tell us about it.

8 What do you think of Gene's explanation for the lack of traffic on their lake: the effort it takes to get there keeps most people away? How have you found that true in your life?

9 The practice Gene described of a parent supporting a child in the water as the child learns to swim is a compelling picture of the way God works in our lives. Based on your observations of people, what's the difference between having God's hands under you and swimming in life on your own? Why are both experiences necessary?

Going Deeper

You can explore the following Bible passages behind the teaching for this session as a group (if there is time) or on your own between sessions.

Read 2 Corinthians 12:7-10. The apostle Paul is often considered the closest thing to the Christian Superman. And yet a glimpse into his daily life reveals a hand that apparently wasn't all that easy to live with. Plus, for God's ambassador to the Gentiles, Paul led a hard life.

- We've never figured out what Paul's specific problem was, but what were the negative effects of this "thorn" on him that this passage talks about?

- Following Paul's example, is it OK to ask God to remove things from our lives that make things difficult or painful? Why did God let Paul ask and then say "No" to his request?

- What lessons about "playing the hand we've been dealt" does this passage give us?

Read John 9:1-12. When we are thinking about the kind of "hand" our lives represent, one of the temptations is to remember all the occasions when we wish we could have experienced a miracle, but nothing happened. Perhaps someone we loved died unexpectedly. Or we were treated unfairly. Or someone was hurt unjustly. And we wonder where God was when that was going on. Greg's second point about God's presence meaning we may be down but not out may sometimes not ring true. This tension may well have been on the disciples' minds as they watched the man who was born blind and then asked Jesus their question.

- The disciples assumed that the man had suffered his fate because someone had sinned. How did Jesus answer their assumption with another possibility?

- Note how this man's understanding of Jesus gradually increased: see vs. 11, 17, 25, 33, 38. This man had been born blind, but what does his experience tell us about the way God actually works in the events of our lives?

- Where does hope come from and how does making room for hope help us face the difficulties of life with endurance and grace?

Sharing Together

Now it's time to make some personal applications to all we've been thinking about in the last few minutes.

10 When you think about the way Joseph coped with and overcame the crushing events in his life, how would you describe your own plan of response to a disappointing or devastating hand in life? How's your approach the same or different compared to Joseph's?

11 When it comes to sustaining hope that keeps you going, what place or role does God have in your life?

12 Describe some instances when God either "held you up" as you were trying to swim or took His hands away as you struggled? What have you learned from those experiences?

During these sessions we are doing things "together:" learning, thinking, growing, praying, choosing, etc. Part of together is how we live when we aren't together. Here are some questions to clarify our shared purposes until we meet again.

13 When you think of your present relationship with Christ, how can the rest of the group be praying for you this week as you seek to give yourself more fully to God's plan (which always includes the possibility of a Joseph-like prison one day and palace the next) in your life?

14 In the last session we asked you to write some names in the Circles of Life diagram. Who did you identify as the people in your life who need to meet Jesus? Go back to the Circles of Life diagram on page 36 to help you think of the various people you come in contact with on a regular basis who need to know Jesus more deeply. Consider the following ideas for action and make a plan to follow through on one of them this week.

- This is a wonderful time to welcome a few friends into your group. Which of the people you listed could you invite? It's possible that you may need to help your friend overcome obstacles to coming to a place where he or she can encounter Jesus. Does your friend need a ride to the group? Help with child care?

- Consider inviting a friend to attend a weekend service with you and possibly plan to enjoy a meal together afterward. This can be a great opportunity to talk with someone about your faith in Jesus.

- Is there someone whom you wouldn't invite to your group but who still needs a connection? Would you be willing to have lunch or coffee with that person, catch up on life and share something you've learned from this study? Jesus doesn't call all of us to lead small groups, but He does call every disciple to spiritually multiply his or her life over time.

Close the session in prayer. Encourage each other to pray audibly for others in the group.

Daily Reflections

These are daily reviews of the key Bible verses and related others that will help you think about and apply the insights from this session.

Day 1

Hebrews 11:1 | Hopeful Faith

Now faith is confidence in what we hope for and assurance about what we do not see. (NIV2011)

What exactly does your faith and hope rely on that you can't see?

Day 2

Genesis 50:19-20 | End of the Story

But Joseph said to them, "Don't be afraid. Am I in the place of God? You intended to harm me, but God intended it for good to accomplish what is now being done, the saving of many lives. (NIV2011)

Our "bad hand" often includes other people. How did Joseph give us a way to forgive others as hope rises?

Day 3

Matthew 19:26 | The Impossible Parachute

Jesus looked at them and said, "With man this is impossible, but with God all things are possible" (NIV 2011).

What difference would it make if you deliberately quoted what Jesus said above more often before giving up on a situation as hopeless or impossible?

Day 4

Hebrews 12:2-3 | When We're Down

Fixing our eyes on Jesus, the pioneer and perfecter of faith. For the joy set before him he endured the cross, scorning its shame, and sat down at the right hand of the throne of God. Consider him who endured such opposition from sinners, so that you will not grow weary and lose heart. (NIV2011)

If the miracle doesn't seem to come quickly enough, how can these verses from Hebrews encourage you to keep hope rising?

Day 5

John 16:1, 33 | Lovingly Warned

All this I have told you so that you will not fall away. . .
I have told you these things, so that in me you may have peace. In this world you will have trouble. But take heart! I have overcome the world. John 16:33 (NIV2011)

Taking heart means applying hope. In what ways do these verses help you deepen your understanding that following Jesus is for a lifetime and beyond?

Weekly Memory Verse

Now faith is confidence in what we hope for and assurance about what we do not see.
Hebrews 11:1 (NIV2011)

Feeling alone and getting to the place of alone comes at us in different ways, as we'll see in the stories of Adrienne, Jeff and Jan. But in those moments when alone comes crashing in, the way God intervenes demonstrates something about His intimate awareness of who we are and what we need.

Session 4

When You Are Facing It Alone

After reading the title, you may be asking, "Facing what alone?". The "it" for each of us is different, and the "it" isn't always the same throughout life. . . but one point of common experience for us has to do with the way we all feel alone when we face challenges. The story from the Bible we looked at last week featured the life of Joseph who spent years essentially alone with the crushing weight of betrayal, abandonment and deceit…yet he thrived. In spite of the hardships, Joseph showed us hope can continue to rise up. Now it's our turn.

Hope is Rising.

By this point we should be settling into a level of comfort with the group, continuing to welcome any newcomers. In this session we'll be taking a look at the subject of facing our solitary moments in life. What can we learn from each other and from God's Word about facing whatever it is, alone?

Coming Together

During each session, we will begin with a question or brief activity designed to "put us on the same page" for the session. Continue to make sure everyone knows names.

1 Being alone or on your own can be, at times, both terrifying and exhilarating. What example(s) of either can you think of from your life?

2 If you've been with us in previous sessions, you know we're aiming at choices and decisions that keep hope rising in our lives. So far, we've talked about shattered plans, life out of control and dissatisfaction with the life-hand we're dealt. In this fourth week, who would like to share a significant personal discovery in one of these areas in your life since we started?

LEARNING TOGETHER

Use the space below for notes, questions or comments you want to bring up in the discussion later.

Growing Together

In the questions that follow, you will review and expand on the teaching you just experienced.

3 Before we take some time for story-telling, what examples come to mind for you that we do live in a society built for two?

4 Just for the fun of it, Gene mentioned Elvis' *Are You Lonesome Tonight* playing on the jukebox at a low point in his life. What other "lonely/alone" songs come to mind?

5 Gene quoted Jesus' words from Matthew 11:28, "Come to me, all you who are weary and burdened, and I will give you rest" (NIV2011). What do you think Jesus meant by those words?

6 What hope do you take away from Gene's comment that the only perfect person who ever lived on Earth was a single guy?

7 People often and rightly focus on Jesus' role as the Son of God who came to Earth to be our Savior. But how significant for you is the idea that Jesus also represents the best pattern or model for living?

8 Gene also mentioned that his Christmas Eve visit to Sam's Town in Las Vegas taught him an important lesson about experiencing being alone. What was the lesson and how does it affect your view of people in your life?

9 Why do you think it's important to know we can "fly solo" or "play solitaire" throughout life and still be normal?

Going Deeper

You can explore the following Bible passages behind the teaching for this session as a group (if there is time) or on your own between sessions.

Read Matthew 11:20-30. This is the context of our memory verse and a key thought for this session: "Come to me, all you who are weary and burdened, and I will give you rest" (Matthew 11:28 NIV2011). Jesus was living and ministering in a society that accepted His amazing miracles but refused to recognize who He was.

- What was Jesus' complaint or charge against the three towns He mentioned in this passage?

- We tend to think of Sodom as the lowest of the low when it comes to societal corruption. Why did Jesus say, "But I tell you that it will be more bearable for Sodom on the day of judgment than for you" (Matthew 11:24 NIV2011)?

- What point is Jesus making in His prayer to His Father in verses 25-26? What does He explain about their relationship in verse 27?

- Verses 28-30 express an invitation from Jesus with significant weight. How would you explain Jesus' statements in your own words?

Read Philippians 3:7-14. Paul had a way of speaking about abandoning everything in order to have a singular focus on the most significant aspect of life, our relationship with God. In this series on hope rising in our lives, it's crucial we understand how hope flows from beyond our day to day experiences. Hope rises and hope reaches.

- How does Paul describe the one thing next to which he calls everything else "a loss" and "rubbish"?

- According to verses 10-11, what is Paul pursuing with a passion?

- How do these verses express a great call to hope without ever using the word?

- What challenges your life in this passage?

Sharing Together

Now it's time to make some personal applications to all we've been thinking about in the last few minutes.

10 Gene invited us to share stories. Sharing stories of our alone or on-our-own experiences allows us to experience the relief of knowing that here and now we are not alone. Let's make this an extended time of storytelling, reflecting on the transparency Gene has demonstrated this session and the previous ones. Who has a story to tell?

11 When we hear someone's story, as Gene pointed out, it can become part of our story. Who can share an insight or encouragement you received from hearing someone else's story in this session?

Going Together

During these sessions we are doing things "together:" learning, thinking, growing, praying, choosing, etc. Part of together is how we live when we aren't together. Here are some questions to clarify our shared purposes until we meet again.

12 Gene closed his teaching with a crucial question: Who can meet the deepest needs of your soul like Jesus says He can? How has your awareness and relationship with Jesus been affected by these sessions?

13 Each of you share how you have done with inviting the people on the Circles of Life to church or your small group.

14 Check in with your spiritual partner(s), or with another partner if yours is absent. Share something God taught you during your time in His Word this week, or read a brief section from your journal. Be sure to write down your partner's progress on page 98.

Daily Reflections

These are daily reviews of the key Bible verses and related others that will help you think about and apply the insights from this session.

Day 1

1 Corinthians 13:13 | Hope's Company

And now these three remain: faith, hope and love. But the greatest of these is love. (NIV2011)

If these three remain, they can rise. But where do they come from and how do you know that?

Day 2

Matthew 11:28-29 | Restful Yoke

[Jesus said:] "Come to me, all you who are weary and burdened, and I will give you rest. Take my yoke upon you and learn from me, for I am gentle and humble in heart, and you will find rest for your souls". (NIV2011)

Based on this week's session, how do you think wearing Christ's yoke would lead to hope rising in you?

Day 3

Romans 5:1-2 | Rejoicing in Rising Hope

Therefore, since we have been justified through faith, we have peace with God through our Lord Jesus Christ, through whom we have gained access by faith into this grace in which we now stand. And we boast in the hope of the glory of God. (NIV2011)

In what ways can you imagine yourself boasting in the hope of the glory of God?

Day 4

Romans 5:3-5 | The Way Hope Rises

Not only so, but we also glory in our sufferings, because we know that suffering produces perseverance; perseverance, character; and character, hope. And hope does not put us to shame, because God's love has been poured out into our hearts through the Holy Spirit, who has been given to us. (NIV2011)

How does this help you understand the way God develops hope in us?

Day 5

Philippians 3:8-9 | Abandon Everything

What is more, I consider everything a loss compared to the surpassing greatness of knowing Christ Jesus my Lord, for whose sake I have lost all things. I consider them rubbish, that I may gain Christ and be found in him, not having a righteousness of my own that comes from the law, but that which is through faith in Christ--the righteousness that comes from God and is by faith. (NIV)

How does Paul help us realize the importance of recognizing what's left when we abandon everything?

Weekly Memory Verse

Come to me, all you who are weary and burdened, and I will give you rest.
(Matthew 11:28 NIV2011)

Giving up is hard to admit and hard to face. In different ways Ian, Jim and Nathan have been at the point of giving up. God did something in each of their lives at that very point. He certainly can do something amazing in our lives, too.

Session 5

When You're About to Give Up

In this session we will look at those moments that come along when we simply don't see a way forward. The grief or the problem or the obstacle seems so great or so strong that we can't imagine a way through. Giving up, bailing out and quitting seem at the moment to be the only choice. And yet, if hope is real, we must take a next step.

If you find yourself facing a "give-it-up" moment, hold that thought until after this session. You may discover that the way forward is right there, but you can't see it quite yet.

Hope is Rising.

Coming Together

During each session, we will begin with a question or brief activity designed to "put us on the same page" for the session.

1 Any bungee jumpers in the group? Who has a story of having to take the plunge (skydiving, rappelling, trust-falling, etc.) or some other situation where you had to go for it when everything inside you was screaming, "No Way!"

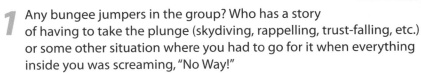

2 If courage is not the absence of fear but the willingness to act, what's the most courageous action you have witnessed someone do?

LEARNING TOGETHER

Use the space below for notes, questions or comments you want to bring up in the discussion later.

Growing Together

In the questions that follow, you will review and expand on the teaching you just experienced.

3 As Gene illustrated with his story of the switched contact lenses, sometimes a little change makes a huge difference. How could you illustrate that principle from your own life?

4 If you had to name one factor in your perspective on life that you sometimes overlook but would never want to forget what would it be? What is the one thing you know always makes a difference if you keep it in mind?

5 What were your first thoughts when Gene got to the part of his story of his friends in Las Vegas whose son was killed in an accident by another boy?

6 Gene described the Psalms of Lament as ancient songs and poems that capture people sounding off on God with shockingly honest feelings, even negative complaints against Him. What do you think about really telling God what's on your mind in your darkest moments?

7 How do you relate with that moment when Jane (the mother of the killed boy) saw the young man who was to blame coming through the receiving line at the funeral?

8 Given a similar situation, what do you think it would take for you to be able to make the right choice between "blessing" or "breaking" that kid?

Going Deeper

You can explore the following Bible passages behind the teaching for this session as a group (if there is time) or on your own between sessions.

Read Joshua 3:14-17. As Gene described the incident, here was a nation ending forty years of wandering in the wilderness about to enter the Promised Land. But there's a huge physical obstacle in the way—the

Jordan River. Forty years previous, they had given up when confronted with a human obstacle (their own fears of the people dwelling in the land). Now they had to face the fear of the flooded river.

- What was the difference between the faith exercised by the priests and the faith exercised by the people as they crossed the Jordan?

- When it comes to taking steps of faith, who are your favorite examples of those who have gone before you?

- Talk together about the lessons in the point Gene made that in order for the river to stop flowing where the priests entered, it had stopped upriver about 18 miles, so the dry bed was on the way before the people got anywhere near stepping into the waters.

Read Psalm 22:1-21. Gene mentioned that one category of Psalms in the Bible is called the Psalms of Lament. About a third of the Psalms fit in this group. The writers certainly had a lot to unload on God. The opening lines of this Psalm are familiar to us as Jesus' words as He hung on the cross.

- Why do you think it's good and healthy for us to be honest with God about what we're feeling and thinking?

- As you read through this Psalm, how many of these lines can you honestly say you would be comfortable expressing to God? Why?

- What do you think Jane had to go through before she reached the place where she could hold Tommy's face and say, "I love you and Jesus loves you, too"?

- How is that entire episode, including Tommy's eventual faith in Christ, an example to you of hope rising?

Sharing Together

Now it's time to make some personal applications to all we've been thinking about in the last few minutes.

9 Who has a "feet dipping in the water of the flooded river" story about God making a way where there seemed to be no way?

10 What difference does it make to you that God has things in motion "18 miles upstream" that you won't see the results of until you step forward in faith?

11 Is there currently a situation in your life you could share with us where you simply can't see a way forward?

Going Together

During these sessions we are doing things "together:" learning, thinking, growing, praying, choosing, etc. Part of together is how we live when we aren't together. Here are some questions to clarify our shared purposes until we meet again.

12 Since this is our next-to-last session in this series, what have we decided about next steps? What area of hopeful living would you like to explore in the future with this or another small group?

13 In what ways would you say this experience has been perhaps preparation for you to lead/host your own small group in the next series?

14 Take a few minutes to discuss the future of your group. How many of you are willing to stay together as a group and work through another study together? If you have time, turn to the Small Group Agreement on page 94 and talk about any changes you would like to make as you move forward as a group.

Close the session in prayer. Encourage each other to pray audibly for others in the group.

Daily Reflections

These are daily reviews of the key Bible verses and related others that will help you think about and apply the insights from this session.

Day 1

Matthew 27:46 | Honest Cry

About three in the afternoon Jesus cried out in a loud voice, "Eli, Eli, lema sabachthani?" (which means "My God, my God, why have you forsaken me?"). (NIV2011)

When was the last time you were completely honest with God? When will you be again?

Day 2

Luke 18:27 | Possibilities

Jesus replied, "What is impossible with man is possible with God." (NIV2011)

In what area(s) of your life are you stretching to give?

Day 3

Genesis 50:19-20 | God's Got the Last Word

But Joseph said to them, "Don't be afraid. Am I in the place of God? You intended to harm me, but God intended it for good to accomplish what is now being done, the saving of many lives." (NIV2011)

Where is a "worst place" in your life where God may be waiting to do something amazing?

Day 4

John 9:25 | New Perspective

He replied, "Whether he is a sinner or not, I don't know. One thing I do know. I was blind but now I see!" (NIV2011)

How has your relationship with Christ changed your view of living?

Day 5

Luke 5:5 | Don't Give Up

Simon answered, "Master, we've worked hard all night and haven't caught anything. But because you say so, I will let down the nets." (NIV2011)

If Jesus tells you to move forward into an impossible situation, what are you going to do?

Weekly Memory Verse

I can do all this through him who gives me strength.
Philippians 4:13 (NIV2011)

Someone said that the secret to prayer is prayer in secret. Talking and thinking about prayer is one thing; actually entering into the space before God in prayer with all that we are is something different. Denise, Greg and Julie have stories to share about why this changes our lives and causes hope to rise.

Session 6

When Your Only Option Is Prayer

"All I can do is pray!"

When someone says that, does it sound like a "hail Mary pass" or plan Z or does it sound like the person is saying, "Well, I've finally realized that whatever I thought I could do to fix this or straighten that out won't work and now it's time to turn it over to someone who has a LOT more resources than I do. It's time for me to get out of the way and let God do what He's been waiting to do all along!"?

Gene will ask us to think seriously about an important issue: why does it take us so long to turn to prayer in the ebb and flow of life?

Hope is Rising.

Coming Together

In this final session of the series we are coming face to face with the choice we have been considering: what kind of life will we live. A life that makes room for God, through the small daily choices, creates space for God to do His work.

1 What would you say is one unforgettable idea that you are taking away from the last five sessions of *Hope Rising*?

2 When you think of the term prayer, what are some specific examples that come to mind?

LEARNING TOGETHER

Use the space below for notes, questions or comments you want to bring up in the discussion later.

Growing Together

In the questions that follow, you will review and expand on the teaching you just experienced.

3 If your group still needs to make decisions about continuing to meet after this session, have that discussion now. Talk about what you will study, who will lead, and where and when you will meet. This conversation is part of your small group mission.

Review your Small Group Agreement on page 94 and evaluate how well you met your goals. Discuss any changes you want to make as you move forward. As your group starts a new study this is a great time to take on a new role or change roles of service in your group. What new role will you take on? If you are uncertain, maybe your group members have some ideas for you. Remember you aren't making a lifetime commitment to the new role; it will only be for a few weeks. Maybe someone would like to share a role with you if you don't feel ready to serve solo.

4 What percentage of your current life do you think has been affected by the sessions we've gone through? In other words, think in terms of percentage and consider how much a sense of rising hope has become a reality in your life over the last six weeks?

5 How did you identify with Gene's admission that because solving problems really turns his crank, coming up against things he can't fix or solve really frustrates him?

6 Gene took us briefly to the last night of Jesus' life and the prospect in front of Him of a terrible experience. Why do you think He prayed? Knowing the suffering was inevitable, He still prayed—how does that affect you?

7 Who is your prayer example? Whom do you know who prays regularly for you?

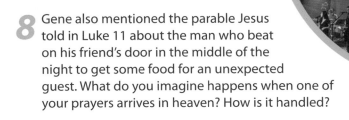

8 Gene also mentioned the parable Jesus told in Luke 11 about the man who beat on his friend's door in the middle of the night to get some food for an unexpected guest. What do you imagine happens when one of your prayers arrives in heaven? How is it handled?

9 If you could have one issue or question really settled about prayer, what would it be?

Going Deeper

You can explore the following Bible passages behind the teaching for this session as a group (if there is time) or on your own between sessions.

Read Luke 11:5-10. Right after Luke's account of Jesus teaching the Lord's Prayer to the disciples, Jesus embarked on an explanatory parable having to do with the necessity and significance of prayer.

- How does this passage cover many of the themes we've touched on in *Hope Rising*?

- Why does the sleepy neighbor agree to supply his persistent friend with bread?

- How does the persistent knocker represent God's expectation of us when it comes to prayer?

- Looking particularly at verses 9-10, does God expect us to try to convince Him or does He want us to exercise persistent faith in the prayer process? Why?

Read Luke 22:39-46. In this passage, Jesus is in the Garden of Gethsemane praying on the night before the cross. Things look hopeless, yet Jesus is praying earnestly. There's no sense that He's going through the motions.

- Twice Jesus tells His disciples, "Pray that you will not fall into temptation" (vs. 40, 46). Why is he warning them that way?

- Based on Luke's shortened account (see also Matthew 26:36-46; Mark 14:32-42), Jesus focused His prayer on one sentence (v.42). What do you notice about this prayer?

- In what ways was this prayer time so much more than Jesus approaching God with a prayer list? How does Jesus' pattern challenge the way we pray?

Sharing Together

At this point we move in our discussion from talking about implications of the teaching to application of the teaching. If we grasp what the idea means we can talk about what it means in our lives.

10 What do you think will need to change in your life in order to demonstrate you understand that a continually developing and deepening prayer life is one of God's primary purposes for your life?

11 Describe to the rest of the group one specific step you are taking to create a tone of prayer without ceasing in your life.

Going Together

During these sessions we are doing things "together:" learning, thinking, growing, praying, choosing, etc. Part of together is how we live when we aren't together. Here are some questions to clarify our shared purposes until we meet again.

12 Below and before you talk about them, take a few minutes to jot down three specific action steps related to this entire series that would move you further on the journey toward hope rising throughout your life. These should be matters others in the group can pray about for you.

a. _____

b. _____

c. _____

13 Now share at least one of these, if not all three, with the rest of the group to create a point of accountability, and give the group permission to ask you about your progress in this or these steps.

Close the session in prayer. Encourage each other to pray audibly for others in the group.

Daily Reflections

These are daily reviews of the key Bible verses and related others that will help you think about and apply the insights from this session.

Day 1

1 Thessalonians 5:16-18 | Non-stop

Rejoice always, pray continually, give thanks in all circumstances; for this is God's will for you in Christ Jesus. (NIV2011)

Why do you think it is God's will for you to pray continually?

Day 2

1 Peter 3:15 | Hopeful Prayer

But in your hearts revere Christ as Lord. Always be prepared to give an answer to everyone who asks you to give the reason for the hope that you have. But do this with gentleness and respect. (NIV2011)

Would someone overhearing your prayer life wonder about the hope you have? Why?

Day 3

Mark 1:35 | Jesus' Pattern

Very early in the morning, while it was still dark, Jesus got up, left the house and went off to a solitary place, where he prayed. (NIV2011)

Why or why doesn't this appeal to you as an obvious way to imitate Jesus?

Day 4

Luke 11:1 | Lord, Teach Us

One day Jesus was praying in a certain place. When he finished, one of his disciples said to him, "Lord, teach us to pray, just as John taught his disciples." (NIV2011)

Why do you think Jesus' disciples made this particular request?

Day 5

James 5:16 | Effective Prayer

Therefore confess your sins to each other and pray for each other so that you may be healed. The prayer of a righteous person is powerful and effective. (NIV2011)

What impact has the honest sharing and praying in your small group had on your life?

Weekly Memory Verse

Rejoice always, pray continually, give thanks in all circumstances; for this is God's will for you in Christ Jesus.
(1 Thessalonians 5:16-18 NIV2011)

Notes

Appendix

Great resources to help make your small group experience even better!

What do we do on the first night of our group?

Like all fun things in life–have a party! A "get to know you" coffee, dinner or dessert is a great way to launch a new study. You may want to review the Group Agreement (page 94) and share the names of a few friends you can invite to join you. But most importantly, have fun before your study time begins.

Where do we find new members for our group?

This can be troubling, especially for new groups that have only a few people or for existing groups that lose a few people along the way. We encourage you to pray with your group and then brainstorm a list of people from work, church, your neighborhood, your children's school, family, the gym and so forth. Then have each group member invite several of the people on his or her list. Another good strategy is to ask church leaders to make an announcement or allow a bulletin insert. No matter how you find members, it's vital that you stay on the lookout for new people to join your group. All groups tend to go through healthy attrition–the result of moves, releasing new leaders, ministry opportunities and so forth–and if the group gets too small, it could be at risk of shutting down. If you and your group stay open, you'll be amazed at the people God sends your way. The next person just might become a friend for life. You never know!

How long will this group meet?

It's totally up to the group–once you come to the end of this six-week study. Most groups meet weekly for at least their first six weeks, but every other week can work as well. We strongly recommend that the group meet for the first six months on a weekly basis if at all possible. This allows for continuity, and if people miss a meeting they aren't gone for a whole month.

At the end of this study, each group member may decide if he or she wants to continue on for another six-week study. Some groups launch relationships for years to come, and others are stepping-stones into another group experience. Either way, enjoy the journey.

Can we do this study on our own?

Absolutely! This may sound crazy but one of the best ways to do this study is not with a full house but with a few friends. You may choose to gather with one other couple who would enjoy going to the movies or having a quiet dinner and then walking through this study. Jesus will be with you even if there are only two of you (Matthew 18:20).

What if this group is not working for us?

You're not alone! This could be the result of a personality conflict, life stage difference, geographical distance, level of spiritual maturity or any number of things. Relax. Pray for God's direction, and at the end of this six-week study, decide whether to continue with this group or find another. You don't buy the first car you look at or marry the first person you date, and the same goes with a group. Don't bail out before the six weeks are up–God might have something to teach you. Also, don't run from conflict or prejudge people before you have given them a chance. God is still working in you, too!

Who is the leader?

Most groups have an official leader. But ideally, the group will mature and members will rotate the leadership of meetings. We have discovered that healthy groups rotate hosts/leaders and homes on a regular basis. This model ensures that all members grow, give their unique contribution and develop their gifts. This study guide and the Holy Spirit can keep things on track even when you rotate leaders. Christ has promised to be in your midst as you gather. Ultimately, God is your leader each step of the way.

How do we handle the child care needs in our group?

Very carefully. Seriously, this can be a sensitive issue. We suggest that you empower the group to openly brainstorm solutions. You may try one option that works for a while and then adjust over time. Our favorite approach is for adults to meet in the living room or dining room, and to share the cost of a babysitter (or two) who can be with the kids in a different part of the house. In this way, parents don't have to be away from their children all evening when their children are too young to be left at home. A second option is to use one home for the kids and a second home (close by or a phone call away) for the adults. A third idea is to rotate the responsibility of providing a lesson or care for the children either in the same home or in another home nearby. This can be an incredible blessing for kids. Finally, the most common idea is to decide that you need to have a night to invest in your spiritual lives individually or as a couple, and to make your own arrangements for child care. No matter what decision the group makes, the best approach is to dialogue openly about both the problem and the solution.

Small Group Agreement

Our Expectations:

To provide a predictable environment where participants experience authentic community and spiritual growth.

Group Attendance	To give priority to the group meeting. We will call or email if we will be late or absent. (Completing the Group Calendar will minimize this issue.)
Safe Environment	To help create a safe place where people can be heard and feel loved. (Please, no quick answers, snap judgments or simple fixes.)
Respect Differences	To be gentle and gracious to people with different spiritual maturity, personal opinions, temperaments or "imperfections" in fellow group members. We are all works in progress.
Confidentiality	To keep anything that is shared strictly confidential and within the group, and to avoid sharing improper information about those outside the group.
Encouragement for Growth	To be not just takers but givers of life. We want to spiritually multiply our life by serving others with our God-given gifts.
Shared Ownership	To remember that every member is a minister and to ensure that each attender will share a small team role or responsibility over time (See the Purpose Team Roles).
Rotating Hosts/ Leaders and Homes	To encourage different people to host the group in their homes, and to rotate the responsibility of facilitating each meeting. (See the Small Group Calendar)

Our Times Together:

• Refreshments/mealtimes _____

• Childcare _____

• When we will meet (day of week) _____

• Where we will meet (place) _____

• We will begin at (time) _____ and end at _____

• We will do our best to have some or all of us attend a worship service together.

  Our primary worship service time will be _____

• Date of this agreement _____

• Date we will review this agreement again _____

• Who (other than the leader) will review this agreement at the end of this

  study _____

Small Group Calendar

Date	Lesson	Host Home	Dessert/Meal	Leader
11/16	1	Steve and Laura's	Joe	Bill

Small Group Roles

The Bible makes clear that every member, not just the small group leader, is a minister in the body of Christ. In a healthy small group, every member takes on some small role or responsibility. It's more fun and effective if you team up on these roles.

Review the team roles and responsibilities below, and have each member volunteer for a role or participate on a team. If someone doesn't know where to serve or is holding back, have the group suggest a team or role. It's best to have one or two people on each team so you have each of the five purposes covered. Serving in even a small capacity will not only help your leader but also will make the group more fun for everyone. Don't hold back. Join a team!

The opportunities below are broken down by the five purposes and then by a crawl (beginning step), walk (intermediate step) or run (advanced step). Try to cover at least the crawl and walk roles, and select a role that matches your group, your gifts and your maturity.

CONNECTING TEAM (Fellowship and Community Building)

Crawl:
Host a social event or group activity in the first week or two.

Walk:
Create a list of uncommitted members and then invite them to an open house or group social.

Run:
Plan a twenty-four-hour retreat or weekend getaway for the group. Lead the Connecting time each week for the group.

GROWING TEAM (Discipleship and Spiritual Growth)

Crawl:
Coordinate the spiritual partners for the group. Facilitate a three- or four-person discussion circle during the Bible study portion of your meeting. Coordinate the discussion circles.

Walk:
Encourage personal devotions through group discussions and pairing up with spiritual (accountability) partners.

Run:
Take the group on a prayer walk, or plan a day of solitude, fasting or personal retreat.

SERVING TEAM
(Discovering Your God-Given Design for Ministry)

Crawl:
Ensure that every member finds a group role or team he or she enjoys.

Walk:
Have every member take a gift test and determine your group's gifts. Plan a ministry project together.

Run:
Help each member decide on a way to use his or her unique gifts somewhere in the church.

SHARING TEAM
(Sharing and Evangelism)

Crawl:
Coordinate the group's Prayer and Praise Report of friends and family who don't know Christ.

Walk:
Search for group mission opportunities and plan a cross-cultural group activity.

Run:
Take a small-group "vacation" to host a six-week group in your neighborhood or office. Then come back together with your current group.

SURRENDERING TEAM
(Surrendering Your Heart to Worship)

Crawl:
Maintain the group's Pray and Praise Report or journal.

Walk:
Lead a brief time of worship each week (at the beginning or end of your meeting), either a cappella or using a song from the DVD or Life Together Worship DVD/CD.

Run:
Plan a unique time of worship through Communion, foot washing, night of prayer or nature walking.

Spiritual Partners' Check-In

Briefly check in each week and write down your personal plans
and progress targets for the next week (or even for the next few weeks).
This could be done (before or after the meeting) on the phone,
through an e-mail message or even in person from time to time.

My Name:

Spiritual Partner's Name:

	Our Plan	Our Progress
Week 1		
Week 2		
Week 3		
Week 4		
Week 5		
Week 6		

Memory Verses

Session 1

But in your hearts revere Christ as Lord. Always be prepared to give an answer to everyone who asks you to give the reason for the hope that you have. But do this with gentleness and respect.
1 Peter 3:15 (NIV2011)

Session 2

The LORD is my shepherd, I lack nothing. He makes me lie down in green pastures, he leads me beside quiet waters, he refreshes my soul. He guides me along the right paths for his name's sake.
Psalm 23:1-3 (NIV2011)

Session 3

Now faith is confidence in what we hope for and assurance about what we do not see.
Hebrews 11:1 (NIV2011)

Session 4

Come to me, all you who are weary and burdened, and I will give you rest.
Matthew 11:28 (NIV2011)

Session 5

I can do all this through him who gives me strength.
Philippians 4:13 (NIV2011)

Session 6

Rejoice always, pray continually, give thanks in all circumstances; for this is God's will for you in Christ Jesus.
1 Thessalonians 5:16-18 (NIV2011)

Prayer and Praise Report

	Prayer Requests	Praise Reports
Session 1		
Session 2		
Session 3		
Session 4		
Session 5		
Session 6		

Group Roster

NAME	ADDRESS	PHONE	EMAIL	MINISTRY	OTHER

EVERYONE

Small Group Leaders

Key resources to help your leadership experience be the best it can be.

Hosting an Open House

If you're starting a new group, try planning an "open house" before your first formal group meeting. Even if you only have two to four core members, it's a great way to break the ice and to consider prayerfully who else might be open to join you over the next few weeks. You can also use this kick-off meeting to hand out study guides, spend some time getting to know each other, discuss each person's expectations for the group and briefly pray for each other.

A simple meal or good desserts always make a kick-off meeting more fun. After people introduce themselves and share how they ended up being at the meeting (you can play a game to see who has the wildest story!), have everyone respond to a few icebreaker questions: "What is your favorite family vacation?" or "What is one thing you love about your church/our community?" or "What are three things about your life growing up that most people here don't know?" Next, ask everyone to tell what he or she hopes to get out of the study. You might want to review the Small Group Agreement and talk about each person's expectations and priorities.

Finally, set an open chair (maybe two) in the center of your group and explain that it represents someone who would enjoy or benefit from this group but who isn't here yet. Ask people to pray about whom they could invite to join the group over the next few weeks. Hand out postcards and have everyone write an invitation or two. Don't worry about ending up with too many people; you can always have one discussion circle in the living room and another in the dining room after you watch the lesson. Each group could then report prayer requests and progress at the end of the session.

You can skip this kick-off meeting if your time is limited, but you'll experience a huge benefit if you take the time to connect with each other in this way.

Leading for the First Time

(Ten common leadership experiences. Welcome to life out in front!)

- Sweaty palms are a healthy sign. The Bible says God is gracious to the humble. Remember who is in control; the time to worry is when you're not worried. Those who are soft in heart (and sweaty palmed) are those whom God is sure to speak through.

- Seek support. Ask your leader, co-leader, or close friend to pray for you and prepare with you before the session. Walking through the study will help you anticipate potentially difficult questions and discussion topics.

- Bring your uniqueness to the study. Lean into who you are and how God wants you to uniquely lead the study.

- Prepare. Prepare. Prepare. Go through the session several times. If you are using the DVD, listen to the teaching segment and Leadership Lifter. Go to www.lifetogether.com and download pertinent files. Consider writing in a journal or fasting for a day to prepare yourself for what God wants to do.

- Don't wait until the last minute to prepare.

- Ask for feedback so you can grow. Perhaps in an email or on cards handed out at the study, have everyone write down three things you did well and one thing you could improve on. Don't get defensive, but show an openness to learn and grow.

- Prayerfully consider launching a new group. This doesn't need to happen overnight, but God's heart is for this to happen over time. Not all Christians are called to be leaders or teachers, but we are all called to be "shepherds" of a few someday.

- Share with your group what God is doing in your heart. God is searching for those whose hearts are fully His. Share your trials and victories. We promise that people will relate.

- Prayerfully consider whom you would like to pass the baton to next week. It's only fair. God is ready for the next member of your group to go on the faith journey you just traveled. Make it fun, and expect God to do the rest.

HOPE RISING

Leadership Training 101

(Top Ten Ideas for New Leaders)

Congratulations! You have responded to the call to help shepherd Jesus' flock. There are few other tasks in the family of God that surpass the contribution you will be making. As you prepare to lead, whether it is one session or the entire series, here are a few thoughts to keep in mind. We encourage you to read these and review them with each new discussion leader before he or she leads.

1. Remember that you are not alone. God knows everything about you, and He knew that you would be asked to lead your group. Remember that it is common for all good leaders to feel that they are not ready to lead. Moses, Solomon, Jeremiah and Timothy—they all were reluctant to lead. God promises, "Never will I leave you; never will I forsake you" (Hebrews 13:5). Whether you are leading for one evening, for several weeks or for a lifetime, you will be blessed as you serve.

2. Don't try to do it alone. Pray right now for God to help you build a healthy leadership team. If you can enlist a co-leader to help you lead the group, you will find your experience to be much richer. This is your chance to involve as many people as you can in building a healthy group. All you have to do is call and ask people to help; you'll be surprised at the response.

3. Just be yourself. If you won't be you, who will? God wants you to use your unique gifts and temperament. Don't try to do things exactly like another leader; do them in a way that fits you! Just admit it when you don't have an answer, and apologize when you make a mistake. Your group will love you for it, and you'll sleep better at night!

4. Prepare for your meeting ahead of time. Review the session and the leader's notes, and write down your responses to each question. Pay special attention to exercises that ask group members to do something other than engage in discussion.

These exercises will help your group live what the Bible teaches, not just talk about it. Be sure you understand how an exercise works, and bring any necessary supplies (such as paper and pens) to your meeting. If the exercise employs one of the items in the appendix, be sure to look over that item so you'll know how it works. Finally, review "Outline for Each Session" so you'll remember the purpose of each section in the study.

5. Pray for your group members by name. Before you begin your session, go around the room in your mind and pray for each member by name. You may want to review the prayer list at least once a week. Ask God to use your time together to touch the heart of every person uniquely. Expect God to lead you to whomever He wants you to encourage or challenge in a special way. If you listen, God will surely lead!

6. When you ask a question, be patient. Someone will eventually respond. Sometimes people need a moment or two of silence to think about the question, and if silence doesn't bother you, it won't bother anyone else. After someone responds, affirm the response with a simple "thanks" or "good job." Then ask, "How about somebody else?" or "Would someone who hasn't shared like to add anything?" Be sensitive to new people or reluctant members who aren't ready to say, pray or do anything. If you give them a safe setting, they will blossom over time.

7. Provide transitions between questions. When guiding the discussion, always read aloud the transitional paragraphs and the questions. Ask the group if anyone would like to read the paragraph or Bible passage. Don't call on anyone, but ask for a volunteer, and then be patient until someone begins. Be sure to thank the person who reads aloud.

8. Break up into small groups each week, or they won't stay. If your group has more than seven people, we strongly encourage you to have the group gather sometimes in discussion circles of three or four people during the SHARING TOGETHER or GOING TOGETHER sections of the study. With a greater opportunity to talk in a small circle, people will connect more with the study, apply more quickly what they're learning and ultimately get more out of it. A small circle also encourages a quiet person to participate and tends to minimize the effects of a more vocal or dominant member. It can also help people feel more loved in your group. When you gather again at the end of the section, you can have one person summarize the highlights from each circle. Small circles are also helpful during prayer time. People who are unaccustomed to praying aloud will feel more comfortable trying it with just two or three others. Also, prayer requests won't take as much time, so circles will have more time to actually pray. When you gather back with the

whole group, you can have one person from each circle briefly update everyone on the prayer requests. People are more willing to pray in small circles if they know that the whole group will hear all the prayer requests.

9. Rotate facilitators weekly. At the end of each meeting, ask the group who should lead the following week. Let the group help select your weekly facilitator. You may be perfectly capable of leading each time, but you will help others grow in their faith and gifts if you give them opportunities to lead. You can use the Small Group Calendar to fill in the names of all meeting leaders at once if you prefer.

10. One final challenge (for new or first time leaders): Before your first opportunity to lead, look up each of the five passages listed below. Read each one as a devotional exercise to help equip yourself with a shepherd's heart. Trust us on this one. If you do this, you will be more than ready for your first meeting.

Matthew 9:36
1 Peter 5:2-4
Psalm 23
Ezekiel 34:11-16
1 Thessalonians 2:7-8, 11-12

Build Community Through Communion

Looking for a wonderful means of worshipping as a group? Why not lead your group in sharing the Lord's Supper? If you've never done this before, the idea certainly seems daunting, but here is a simple form by which your small group can share this sacrament. Of course, churches vary in their treatment of Communion so you may need to adapt these suggestions to your church's beliefs.

Steps in Serving Communion

1 Out of the context of your own experience, say something brief about God's love, forgiveness, grace, mercy, commitment, tenderheartedness or faithfulness. Connect your words with the personal stories of the group. For example, "These past few weeks I've experienced God's mercy in the way He untangled the situation with my son. And I've seen God show mercy to others of us here, too, especially to Jean and Roger." If you prefer, you can write down ahead of time what you want to say.

2 Read 1 Corinithians 11:23-26*: The Lord Jesus, on the night he was betrayed, took bread, and when he had given thanks, he broke it and said, "This is my body, which is for you; do this in remembrance of me." In the same way, after supper he took the cup, saying, "This cup is the new covenant in my blood; do this, whenever you drink it, in remembrance of me." For whenever you eat this bread and drink this cup, you proclaim the Lord's death until he comes.

3 Pray silently, and pass the bread around the circle. While the bread is being passed, you may want to reflect quietly, sing a simple praise song or listen to a worship song.

4 When everyone has received the bread, remind them that this represents Jesus' broken body on their behalf. Simply state, "Jesus said, 'Do this in remembrance of me.' Let us eat together," and eat the bread as a group.

5 Pray silently, and serve the cup. You may pass a small tray, serve people individually or have them pick up a cup from the table.

6 When everyone has been served, remind them that the cup represents Jesus' blood shed for them. Simply state, "The cup of the new covenant is Jesus Christ's blood shed for you. Jesus said, 'Do this in remembrance of me.' Let us drink together." Then drink the juice as a group.

7 Conclude by singing a simple song or listening to a praise song, or having a time of prayer in thanks to God.

Practical Tips in Serving Communion

1 Prepare the elements simply, sacredly and symbolically.

2 Be sensitive to timing in your meeting.

3 Break up pieces of cracker or soft bread on a small plate or tray. Don't use large servings of bread or grape juice. You should think about using grape juice—and not wine—because alcohol may be an issue for some people.

4 Have all of the elements prepared beforehand, and just bring them into the room or to the table when you are ready.

Here are some other good Communion passages: Matthew 26:26-29, Mark 14:22-25, Luke 22:14-20, 1 Corinthians 10:16-21 or 1 Corinthians 11:17-34.

Gene Appel

Gene Appel, Senior Pastor of Eastside Christian Church, Anaheim, CA, began his ministry as a 20-year-old intern at Eastside. After moving on to pastor two of the largest churches in the nation—Central Christian Church, Las Vegas, NV and Willow Creek Community Church, South Barrington, IL—he returned in 2008 to lead Eastside into its next chapter. Since that time Eastside has become one of America's fastest growing churches and relocated in November of 2012 from Fullerton to a new campus in Anaheim.

Following in the footsteps of his late father, a pastor and Christian leader, Gene sensed God's call on his life to ministry at an early age. He received a B.A. degree in Preaching Ministry from Lincoln Christian University and has done additional graduate work at Lincoln and Hope International University, which also conferred upon him an honorary Doctor of Divinity in 2011.

Known to his friends and colleagues as a leader, creative Bible teacher, author and leadership coach, Gene served for 18 years as senior pastor of Central Christian Church, Las Vegas. Under his leadership Central grew from 450 to 8,000 in its services weekly and relocated to a 56-acre campus in 1999. During this period Central transitioned from a fairly traditional ingrown and declining church to one strategically focused on reaching and discipling non-churched people. Additionally, Gene was instrumental in planting two other of Las Vegas' most dynamic churches and began coaching church leaders domestically and internationally on leading churches through healthy change.

In 2003, Gene became a part of the team at Willow Creek Community Church in South Barrington, IL where he served as lead pastor working alongside senior pastor, Bill Hybels. Gene's responsibilities included serving as a teaching pastor and bringing focused vision and leadership to the South Barrington congregation and staff. Gene also served as a member of the Willow Creek elder board and board of directors.

While at Willow Creek Gene continued to teach and mentor church leaders globally through the Willow Creek Association. He also was a weekly commentator on WBBM-TV for 4 years, the CBS television affiliate in Chicago, providing spiritual insights on local, national and world events. Gene was recognized for his work by the Illinois Broadcasting Association with the Silver Dome award for best editorial/commentary in the state of Illinois.

Eastside Christian Church has a vision to reach 1% of the 5.8 million people who live within 20 miles of its campus, including a special emphasis on the growing Latino population of Southern California. Eastside is known as a church that pursues God, builds community and unleashes compassion, next door, locally and globally.

Gene is the co-author of the book, *How to Change Your Church… without Killing It*, and also authored *Dream Intruders* and *Healing Hidden Hurts*.

Gene and his wife Barbara met in Las Vegas and are the parents of three children—Jeremy, Alayna and Jenna. His hobbies include boating, fishing, water-skiing, jet-skiing and anything else that can be done on or near water.